Drowned Lands

THE
James
DICKEY
CONTEMPORARY POETRY SERIES

EDITED BY RICHARD HOWARD

Drowned Lands

Poems by
Paul Kane

UNIVERSITY OF SOUTH CAROLINA PRESS

Published in Columbia, South Carolina, by the
University of South Carolina Press

Manufactured in the United States of America

04   03   02   01   00   5   4   3   2   1

Library of Congress Cataloging-in-Publication Data

Kane, Paul, 1950–
    Drowned lands : poems / by Paul Kane.
      p.   cm. — (The James Dickey contemporary poetry series)
    ISBN 1-57003-340-4 (alk. paper) —
    ISBN 1-57003-341-2 (pbk. : alk. paper)
    I. Title.   II. Series.
    PS3561.A4715 D76   2000
    811'.54—dc21   00-010792

Poems in this book were first published in the following magazines and jour-
nals: *Arena Magazine*, "In the Penal Colony"; *Bookpress*, "Epicurean"; *New
Criterion*, "Iconoclastics" part iii—"Untitled"; *New Republic*, "*Wis-
senschaftslehre*"; *Paris Review*, "*Concedo Nulli*," "Letter of the Prophet
Mohammed," "Q & A," "Framing," "The Repentant Magdalen," "Time
Was," "Mere Islands," "Disciples Asleep at Gethsemane"; *Poetry*, "Varia-
tions on a Stanza by Longfellow"; *poetry etc*, "Flight from the Present," "At
the Terminus"; *Quadrant*, "Outback Before Dawn," "Under the Iron Rain-
bow"; *The Rialto*, "Salt Level"; *Salt*, "Kakadu Memory," "On the Murray";
Voices, "Under the Summer Canopy"; *Western Humanities Review*, "An
Old Flame in Savonarola's Cell," "Iconoclastics" part i—"The Heavenly
Ladder of Johannes Climacus," "Prelude," "After Martial," "Shadows."

NATIONAL
ENDOWMENT
FOR THE ARTS

Publication of this book was supported by a grant from the
National Endowment for the Arts.

For Tina

Ô! J'ai lieu de louer!

St.-John Perse

The falling waters led me,
The foodful waters fed me,
And brought me to the lowest land . . .

Emerson

Contents

A Note on Paul Kane

Just over a decade ago, Joseph Brodsky called the poems of Kane's first book of verse "disturbingly quiet . . . mesmerizing in their opaqueness, about what it is like for us to live 'so far beneath the sky,'" and mentioned the "dark echo of Robert Frost sounded (and heard) in the poetry. The words seem even more prescient and precise in the mouth of a dead man—only Brodsky would evoke a *dark* echo, as if Frost were not sufficiently umbrageous for Kane, for himself, and for poetry. In that book which Brodsky's comment adumbrates, I had occasion to "introduce" the poet with a sort of reader's quandary (which Brodsky was quite in accord with, quite happy to share): could anything this deliberately amiable be so amiable as all that?

Ten years later, another forty-some poems clear up—if they do not clarify—my predicament: what is so reader-friendly at the start is by such means bound and determined to get to the bottom of the matter, the fact that we "ache with an alien solitude, knowing what / changes us flows from a sea beyond change." Kane had observed that his title poem "gestured toward" the netherworld of the *Aeneid,* where the unburied dead reach out toward the farther shore. And now *Drowned Lands* completes, if it does not conclude, the story. "The sound dies down / and lifts again," the systole and diastole of mortality itself wonderfully resumed and retracted, living away, dying back.

It is to be noticed, in this gently *manifesting* poet, that one need not beat a big drum or sound a brazen trumpet in order to solicit elemental energies. After the farther shore, the immersed territory is revealed, quietly indeed, but the more capably for that, "to fill the reasonable shore / that now lies foul and muddy," as Prospero says, exercising another such spell. Kane extends the magic, for he by now reveals himself as a poet of geological figuration, a modest apocalypst with a far from modest claim upon our physical, our metaphysical, our *religious,* intentions:

We will be here, part of the land, part
of the whole flowing inland sea-wash

from which we emerged differentiated.
The earth holds much in store for us . . . .

Everything we do goes against the grain,
which is why, in the first place, we do

anything at all. In the Drowned Lands only
the ditch has meaning, for it gives rise

to the unnatural purpose of rising above
our means to attain in time our end.

One no longer "introduces" such a poet, nor notes "development";
it is a matter now (however mannerly) of functioning powers, and
for the reader, of poems fulfilled.

RICHARD HOWARD

I

Time Was

The Mood of Glass

How sunlight brightens the mood of glass:
burnishing this world, inside and out,
delighting what windows encompass.

It is afternoon under the hemlock;
it is morning here, with louvered shadows
and the frantic ticking of a wound-up clock.

But the glass, undeceived, sees through it all,
mirroring the mood, bringing it to light—
its motive, by turns, transparent and opaque.

Cross Lots

Across the tree-lined street (where curbside in autumn we raked
  and burned our piles of leaves—learning then how to play with fire),
down the dirt driveway between the neighbor's barn and a high
  wooden fence overhung with branches and thick climbing vines
(protecting the lonely woman who spied on us all day),
  over the path through underbrush (where we played out dramas
contrived from the fantastic trauma of adolescence),
  then onto the level backyard of the neighbor's neighbors
(who were old and kind and never complained of the trespass—
  so we skirted their gardens and never did them mischief),
crossing behind their house and driveway to Clinton Circle
  and through the circle, with its trellised garden and stonework
(a public space no one used except late at night),
  then a sprint over the sloping lawn of the angry man
(never reconciled to the fate of serving the Short-Cut),
  quick, onto his stone wall, and a jump to my friend's front yard
where they harvested dandelions and made yellow wine
  (his dad owned a hunting bow with razor arrows for deer,
but we could hardly bend the bow and so learned a man's strength),
  over the bridge over the creek (under which torment ruled
when we played at building dams and searched for tadpoles and frogs),
  then up the paved road by the small courthouse of the J.P.
to Grand Street, with its oversized houses and mansard roofs,
  down Chapel Street, by the Lutheran Church of the high steeple
(whose golden ball on top looked skewered like a shish kebab),
  entering the grounds of the undertaker's establishment,

all red brick with creamy trim and immaculate manicured lawns
  (but in the cellar, the bodies his son would help prepare),
right to the back of the property to the path across
  the long vacant lot (where once I cornered a startled deer
and then became the frightened one, facing desperation),
  up and stumbling down the uneven path, kicking aside
milkweed and burdock, kelpweed and thistle, and chicory
  and Queen Anne's lace—wild carrot, bird's nest of wasted ground
(where I ran after butterflies but found them mere insects dead),
  then, the gravel parking lot across from the library
of the high ceilings, strange rituals and hushed silences
  (seeming more a place of worship, more ancient than it was),
and finally up the street, turning left through the iron gate
  into the courtyard and playground of the imposing school—
where daydreams stopped and humiliating knowledge began.

Acceptance

Gray across the bridge, the bridge
itself silver, shining in the dull air,

the gray mist and water below
pale, obscuring any view but

the prevalent neutrality. Gray, then,
with splashed color, lights moving

slowly, the bridge trafficking in
anonymous lives, sequestered worlds—

it could be this way always, somber
and yet not sad: washed, toned down,

quiet, even serene. It would be
all right, with much still to praise.

An Old Flame in Savonarola's Cell

Florence, May 1971

What possessed me to pry into the cell
of the old preacher, so richly repaid in

the bonfire of his own vanity? And what
vain desire drove me to pursue, a year

before, her who stood there hanging fire
at my abashed hello? I cannot even recall

her name now, barely even her face, but
the encounter itself remains indelible

in its effect, like a dream that fades upon
waking but colors the whole morning blue.

Memories fall from us years later like
scales from the eyes. As life unravels, Fate—

that bad seamstress—rips what we sew.
Then, it was the sophomoric poems I regretted

most, the inanity of all that inanition, as if
composure were comprehended by a pose.

She was gracious enough in the end, and
though I burned with awkward shame

the cloister could not have been colder—as
she swept past me out of the cell—than on

any day in spring when an icy wind came down
the Arno and pried into the Dominican's heart.

Framing

Header, plate, bracket, joist, and brace—
words nailed into place

in the grammar of the addition.
It all adds up, as each edition

of the plan is issued daily
over morning coffee. Rarely

does our thinking match what yesterday
came clear as the day

before. This protean porch has gone
from screen to glass along

the imagined way to its present form:
all open air, framed in two-by-fours

through which sky and field
are ordered by words that yield

structure and a sense of place:
header, plate, bracket, joist, and brace.

By the Hudson

Whitecaps running south,
March winds billowing southwest,
and it is cold still.

Trucks bear down Route 9,
reverberating through the house:
a rumbling heartburn.

I've had my fill,
winter's drip and drizzle, icy stares—
spring, be warm as wool.

Just after the Holidays

The man across the street was marked out by death,
though he had a second life after his first heart attack.

I remember him one afternoon transformed by a laugh
into someone only his wife would have recognized years before.

He quit his job to take up his life, his family—
he took up jogging too—he was glad he was alive.

Death for him was a red pickup truck skidding:
it climbed a snowy embankment to get at him,

and though he ran for his life, he lost it there
that morning, just after the holidays.

Shadows

i
A ribbon of cloud billows in the valley,
An opaque mirror of the river below.
You are crossing a bridge in sunlight,
Suspended above cloud, water, ground.
        And do you remember such moments?

ii
On an overcast day, a patch of sun
Brightens a far corner of the field.
It passes like a shadow in the wind,
A negative of the positive world.
        And do you come to yourself just then?

iii
As the wake pursues the boat, the water
Enfolds the sky in the swell of the waves.
You drink the light in, as you would the air,
In deep breaths, in dilations of time.
        And do you know what it is to live?

The Cipher

17,702
subtracted from my
sum of days—that zero, a
ball bounding down an incline
and I rushing to catch it in my arms:
a lost lover I never thought to meet
again. As different as midnight is to
noon, on to off, one plus minus-one
equals an integer I cannot calculate
except by a too transparent
figuring, a division from
a whole.

A Bouquet for Elizabeth

for E. Riley

Every time I walk down this street, I
Recall that day: looking over your books
In the old apartment, with its sunny nooks,
Listening to the trilling lilt in your voice—
Each time I hit upon a favorite, you'd rejoice,
Yielding it up, the way blossoms open to the sky.

Driving East

In the violet dawn, clouds stretched across clouds
layer the light, and near the sunrise, soot.

The colorless foliage awaits its
differentiation: red, orange, yellow

and the overall green to inhabit
the eye. In the east, the first fire ignites

the horizon line, our destination.
Lit from below, we are what we behold.

In the distance, Breakneck Ridge, mistaken
for banks of cloud, glows distinct: violet shifts

to purple, and the revealed world burns.
It is the risen sun blots out the sky.

Cats at the Protestant Cemetery

From one end of Rome to
the other, was there time?
From Vaticano to Piramide and
   back like a perfect rhyme?

I took my chances that
last day in Rome—call it
a pilgrimage, a desire to mark the day in
   homage to holy writ.

There was no mistaking
the tomb of Cestius—
though even Hardy's poem hadn't prepared me for
   that marble colossus.

Down the narrow via,
I guessed which gate to try:
it opened from within as I drew near, as if
   in greeting to my good-bye.

Little signs showed the way:
up to Shelley, over
to Keats, Trelawney, Symonds—
   expatriates in clover.

Shelley's grave stoical,
Keats's bitter with loss,

but in the cool green Protestant shade, what could be
    more serene than pathos?

    And then the feral cats
    appeared, a score or so
like the genius loci of all that genius
    roaming the cimitero.

    What could I do but stop,
    speak to the attentive
one that brushed against my leg: Are you Goethe's son?
    Yowl was negative.

    Still, something unearthly
    mingled with the feline
grace of those cemetery cats, as if in Rome
    there's nothing not divine.

Epicurean

after Horace, *Odes* 3.13

O Wheeler Creek, clear as ice cubes in a glass,
you are worth all the pretty flowers and fruits
    that grow nearby for all the watery sounds
        you make here on the garden's verge

at day's end—in midsummer—amid life's hurry.
In the morning feral cats and at dusk the raccoon
    drink by your streaming edge, but we
        would never drink your waters

for the farms above have fertilized you beyond
human delectation. Elegant horses in paddocks,
    cows in common pastures, do not appreciate
        you more than we, who only admire

your good looks and voice—like Lynda, that blonde
Parisian soap star from Perth, whose perfections
    were as sweet as Sauternes at evening
        by your side, O Wheeler Creek.

Mona

Mona, alone, and the thick clouds rise
in the distance like plumes from a fire,

and the blue, steel-blue, of the sky
rolls back the sense of closeness,

and Mona, alone, thinks that time
is the shifting distances of the heart,

that time alone is no great help when
you are Mona, not wishing for solitude,

but full of the hope of the bright sky,
which is time, turning over, turning over,

in the magnanimity of indifference
that leaves you alone, for you are

Mona, alone. That is you.

Intimations

At the point where we depend
on the independence of each

other, something else occurs:
a tangled clearing in the woods,

a sudden cascade in the stream,
a flushed bird rising.

We go separate ways,
and always come together

on the basis of our need:
light, greenness, each other.

Prelude

A breeze through the open window stirs
the smell of cedar shingles in the shed:
    this day is prelude to all the rest.
    Shadows of birds move through
the twisted leaves of the tree above.
The birds call constantly to one another.

The wind is soundless, only leaves and branches
give it voice in this end-of-summer afternoon.
    The sway and swish of the giant
    willow is kelp-like in mimic motion,
riding currents we feel but do not see.
We see so little what touches our concern.

Time is a wind we are moved by—we measure it
by the rule of sorrow: increment, sovereignty, law,
    autonomous in nothing but death.
    Everything alien dies with us:
what is left is what we have left. Alone, we
look to ourselves and see the world around us.

Under the Summer Canopy

In a haze of cloud that drifts among the trees,
birds dart between branches, between cries.

The stream runs through the scale of its music,
over stones, tree roots, and around the downward bend.

Against a backdrop of gray, insects reverberate,
as the garden diminishes in shades of sere.

Under the canopy of summer sky we turn
to leave—a gesture appropriate to our time.

Time Was

Still, I must not forget that I once managed to put these things into writing.

Blanchot

When the high-pitched sounds of the August continuo
circulated like breezes through the immovable heat,
time was a single leaf drifting upwards, then down.

In the emptying out, the vacating of routine,
the laboring fullness came to pass, and became,
in passing, what went before and never came again:

the bellflower, blue against the lichened rock,
the sudden oriole in the cherry tree,
the offhand remark indelible in the mind.

In the morning within the morning, in the midnight
within the noon, word echoed within word—
while the mockingbird sang a palindrome of time.

Between the background of the body, and the fore-
shortened space of speech, we lived in the middle distance
where time was, and was not—where we are living still.

II

Drowned Lands

Drowned Lands

The Black Dirt

> This immense surface when entirely dry will become the principal
> source of riches in these districts.
>
> Hector St. John de Crèvecoeur

The crop duster, sun-bright yellow against the blue sky,
dips low along the black-dirt flats verdant with neat rows—
onions, celery, lettuce, cabbage, white and red potatoes—
then climbs steeply, scaling the air, revolving dance-like,
a slow serene spin around an invisible axis.
    The wide bands of muckland are hemmed by hills
    and dotted with limestone islands, forested, peopled,
    though once grated white by glaciers leaving lake beds
    behind, when all this took shape in the unforgotten time.

The "Real Men," the Delaware Lenni-Lenape, left shards
in caves, arrowheads in fields, names everywhere elided now.
Cranberries and walnuts drew them but the soil held them
along the Wallkill River and the flood plains full of cedars.
Only birds and spirits then inhabited the impossible sky.
    Sky and land were sold for a song, which became an anthem
    and then a dirge when the English made it a hymn—whose
    strains we hear now in the rise and fall of the yellow biplane
    humming in the distance like something unremembered.

There are five layers of soil if you dig down through
the black dirt to the red-brown fibrous sections

and further to the denser gray and whitish-gray claypan.
The decay of sedge under a film of standing water imbued
the dreams of men with primordial drives, like dreams.
     "Nature, as if to banish nudity, had embellished
     this immense plain with several islands of different sizes,
     the land of which was extremely fertile"—so Crèvecoeur
     wrote, watering the dream again with words.

1773, and the Legislature seeks to raise money to raise
the Drowned Lands, and two years later tries again.
But it was a hundred years of migration that drained first
the old world and then the swamps—Poles, Germans, Irish—
yet that is a story the land knows well and repeats endlessly.
     Chickens and goats make a brisk trade in summer, as migrants
     work the sacramental fields: Blacks, Puerto Ricans, Mexicans,
     and the Haitians with their voodoo and patois—the rites
     of summer are complex here, more rights than wrongs.

Dig deep enough, you drain the soil; dig deeper and the floods
run off. What then are we left with? Resurrected lands?
Mile after mile of green that holds the black, except
in a dry winter when the wind lifts the fine-grained dirt
and the coal-black dust insinuates under doors and windows.
     In early spring the seed onions bloom like pom-poms,
     and late snow—the poor man's fertilizer—makes
     a garden of pure white between the green blush of the hills
     and the darker islands. Seedtime brings the yellow biplane.

ii
Language of Flowers
     Farming is magical: I plant alfalfa and I get dandelions.
                              local farmer (Warwick, NY)

Every year we reclaim the garden from growth
gone wild, and every year it stakes its claim again:
mustard seed, wild phlox, forget-me-not, fleabane—all

speak a florid language in rebuke: Indifference, Unanimity,
True Love, Variety; even the dandelion is an Oracle.

But a garrulous nature confuses the issue—profusion
in the service of what? A sprawling self-regard?
We prune and hack and dig, treating all weeds as verbs,
replacing them with the proper nouns we choose:
Impatiens, Vinca, Iris, Morning Glory, Sunflower, Cosmos.

In the evening we sit in the eye of the storm, complacent,
serene, as if it were we who were growing so naturally
on water, sunlight, and the nutrients of the humus.
We plant ourselves in the garden, in our green chairs,
and scrutinize the hours with a practiced eye.

What was it like to be alive this golden day?
We hardly know, except moment by moment when
the minute hand stops on the kitchen clock or
the seconds divide. What time is it? As if
there were many kinds of time to discern.

Time to go in, time to get up, time to get going—
these are the parts of speech nature leaves out
in the headlong cyclic surge we call the World.
How are we to survive? We drain, irrigate, till,
we sow and harvest—we celebrate and so live.

iii
Salt Level

> "My dreams!
> I only put them down for a minute!"
>> Philip Hodgins (Maryborough, Australia)

Here, in a parched land, the red soil is dry, is dust,
save where they irrigate the vineyards and crops,
or water lawns and the emerald public parks.

The slow shallow river, muddy with carp, drops—
      but the salt level rises.

We are here with friends to celebrate an occasion
which masks another event we anticipate
now as coming too soon, for the chemo can't stop
the rage of cell against cell, and still you participate—
      though the salt level rises.

Trees are pumps, you explain, the leaves evaporate
the moisture drawn by the roots, and it is this toil
which keeps the water table steady, the land intact.
But they have cut down the trees, despoiling the soil—
      for the salt level rises.

It catches us at odd moments, each one separately,
the loss we face. You don't deny it's more than grim
but, making it your own, turn it to poems to outstrip
you. Now our wells cannot empty fast enough and brim—
      when the salt level rises.

iv
Aftermath

> It seems that large bodies such as these are subject, as are our own,
> to changes, some natural, some feverish.
>
>   Michel de Montaigne

They will return someday, the glaciers,
whether as ice or fire-melted water,

return and remake the land, changing it
back to an outcrop of limestone and granite.

We will be here, part of the land, part
of the whole flowing inland sea-wash

from which we emerged differentiated.
The earth holds much in store for us.

Clouds now are piling up in the distance
and darkening. Patches of blue, tufted

around the edges, allow just enough sun
to give a sheen to the last light withdrawing.

If it should rain, the ground will absorb it
and send the runoff to the streams, rivers, sea.

Everything we do goes against the grain,
which is why, in the first place, we do

anything at all. In the Drowned Lands only
the ditch has meaning, for it gives rise

to the unnatural purpose of rising above
our means to attain in time our end.

At Witter Bynner's House

> He was naturally so sensitive, and so kind. But he had the insidious
> modern disease of tolerance.
>
> D. H. Lawrence

The earth-pink adobe and turquoise trim
take the light, but return no memory of him

who, even now, lives by virtue of the letter—
someone who knew everyone no better

than himself. "Now flay me," he wrote Lorenzo,
stung by the Plumed Serpent's wicked tale—and so,

in the dry and droll air, friendship withered
to a sere garden that has not weathered

an August drought. In the end, the genial Bynner
turned, and slowly turned, unwittingly bitter.

Wissenschaftslehre

In short, there is for me absolutely no such thing as an existence that
has no relation to myself.

Johann Gottlieb Fichte (Berlin, 1800)

"Himself as everything! How does Mrs. Fichte
    put up with it?"—so Heine jokes, yet forgets she
exchanged her sickbed for a deathbed, infecting
    Mr. Fichte with the typhus got tending to
her ethics among the poor. And he—of the un-
    bending will, son of a ribbon maker, and a
tender of geese—wore out his *Willkomm* among lax
    professors, dueling students, and Goethe himself!
Who could blame the Visiting Spirit for smiting
    him to the ground, who could only respond, "but you
refer me to myself"? As Napoleon neared
    Berlin, the *philosophe* fled, vowing to raise the
avenging spirit of the German *Volk*, for by
    then the Science of Knowledge was history. Five
years after his death, they buried Mrs. Fichte,
    laying her by his side—dust to dust, all to all.

Burning the Flag

Empty, engulfed, the container sits
on the road, while flames billow
in the colors of the flag.
People watch in disbelief,
as smoke and soot choke the air.

It is 1963.
Wrapt in his immolation—
an enormous robe swept
by the wind—the Buddhist monk
burns on the streets of Saigon.

It is still 1963.
Flames lick at the corrupted
body, as if seeking a soul. It is fled.
The air around fills with cries.
They are burning the flag again.

War Crimes

Under siege, the shot
you don't hear
is the one that kills you.

After Martial

A drop of venom, a little bit of gall.

Martial Epigrams 7.25

i

So, Juventius, you think that by splitting hairs
you can occult the bald truth—or rather bold-faced
ruse—as if closing your eyes at night disappears
the room? Your choplogic *tonton macoutes* lay waste

to honest effort and plain struggling self-respect.
Don't smile at me your insipid grin, strutting past
in your peacock walk all pigeon-toed: your aspect
is aspic—not even Lycaon would serve you for breakfast.

ii

Mr. Backbone sees two sides to every question:
his and yours, but—like the jellyfish—prefers to ride
the tides, if only he could read the currents

aright and figure which way the wind will run.
Pulled in different directions, he'd rather hide
but seems to have slipped a disk climbing the fence.

iii

Ms. Frisson's apolitical but not unemotional,
her sense of self-deception purely notional.

Buy into me, she says, I'm so sincere,
when you see no evil there's nothing to fear.

iv

Tell me, where in the forum, Simplissima,
did you gain such purchase on ambition?
It's a hard currency you deal in these days—
when you talk of openness, I get agoraphobia.

v

God of doorways, thresholds, past and future,
cold month's namesake, frozen in time:
speak Januarius, don't lock it away—rust
and the moth aren't the only ways to decay.

Incident in the Barnyard

Monsieur Hirsute is a mere youth
under his beard—his outbreaks of temper
the playground transports of a bully.

Offer him insults or correction,
he rages red-faced and puffed up,
a swaggering turkey cock crying foul.

Feathers smoothed, his unctuous regret
is more distasteful yet, the sincere clucks
of self-delusion, chicken to the egg hypocrisy.

Letter of the Prophet Mohammed

Alexandria, A.D. 627

"From Mohammed, the Servant and Prophet of Allah,
    to Muqavas, Leader of the Copts: There is
safety and security for those believers who
    follow the correct path."
                              *—This I believe, but
danger and uncertainty follow as surely,
    for why else should this sudden burden fall now?
Who would wish to prove a prophet false?*
                                        "Thus I invite
    you to accept Islam. If you accept it,
then you shall find security, save your throne, and gain
    twice as much reward for having introduced
Islam to your people."
                          *—Is this not magnanimous?
    And if I were to gain twice as much and lose
my soul, and those souls rendered unto me as bishop?
    What invitation ever invites reward?
Do I dine with friends upon expectation?*
                                        "If you
    refuse this invitation, then let the sin
of calamity which awaits your followers be
    upon you."
                *—Now I know the man's character.
If calamity be a sin, then good fortune is
    mere grace and not a thing I accept or no.
My followers follow whom I follow.*

39

"You too are
People of the Book. Therefore, let us come to
a Word Common between us, that we worship none but
Allah and shall not equalize anything
with Him. Let us not abandon Allah, let us not
take others for lords other than Him."
                                        —*And what
*is that word but Word made flesh? I know not Allah and
equalize him with nothing. His Book has no
word for charity. See, he closes:*
                                        "If you do not
consent to this invitation, bear witness
that we are Muslims."
                        —*This too I readily believe,
for when the storm wind lifts the sand there is no
resisting—we hide our faces and seek out shelter.
I'll write this man and indulge his messenger.*

To Mohammed, the Servant and Prophet of Allah,
    my greetings. I am aware that a Prophet
is yet to arise, but I am of the opinion
    that he will appear in al Sham. *(I would not
anger this man beyond reason. He will know Coptic
    seers point to Syria.)* Your messenger
has been received with honor. *(Hatib ibn Balta'ah
    will carry a good report of Egyptian
beneficence. Kindness now may bring kindness later,
    and mercies.)* I send for your acceptance two
sisters, highly valued among the Copts, a present
    of raiment, and a mule for you to ride on .
*(I have word of his taste for wives. Shirin and Mary
    will slave for him too. Better that such beauty
be in the service of need. And Duldul, the white mule—
    that will be a fine rarity. I'll send him
a donkey as well and coin tribute.)* I would accept
    your invitation but I am a leader

40

and cannot do as I might wish. *(True enough. Egypt*
  is a land of martyrs and Monophysites
and the two are not dissevered under Byzantine
  rule. There may be one God but there are many
swords.) May you prosper in your faith, Your humble servant
  in the Lord, —Muqawqis, Leader of the Copts.
(Where is the correct path if all is devastation?)

Eurydice

Orpheus? How is it he does not hear me?
    I call out and my O is a hole
in the air I make with my mouth. *Orpheus.*
    If he would once look upon my face
he would understand it is not life he leads
    me to—my death was the death of us.
Why does he take me from my oblivion?
    This wind on my cold back drives me, but
how—you gods—can he draw me after him this way?
    Already I see the light I hoped
never to see again. *Stop*. If he cannot
    hear me, surely he feels me behind
him. Am I not the ache in his heart, the doubt
    in his mind? *Turn, Orpheus*. Release me.

Frost, at Midnight

i
Frost
Midnight comes and is gone—day swung shut on
the hinge of night—another day opening
in darkness, but for the lamp's double cone
of light: above on the ceiling, below
on the desk—an hourglass measuring unblessed
moments of silence, solitude and thought.
A book lies open, taking the measure
of the world, of what in dreams is sought or
found in the fissure that separates and
joins two translucent worlds of fire and ice—
the red and blue of what sunsets conceal.
Estrangements of beauty suffice now as
images of what's revealed in a book.
A killing frost is forecast in the clear
lit sky, black frost that levels the garden
gone to seed—the last life before all is
lost in rich decay. We are as strangers
in this realm, even as we make it our
own, even as it claims us for its own.
At night we dream, and in daylight, we see
as through rippled film, or old glass or thin
imperfect ice—we feel how permeable
the world is, how the world is not unreal.

ii

At Midnight

The house is abed, and in the quiet,
small sounds magnify: the little clock ticks
on the shelf, the water heater whispers
in the basement, while the wind scrapes a branch
against the siding. Silence: an absence
we never allow for, for very long.
Outside, the coldest night yet of the year.
Stars withdraw as the moon whitens the sky
and the new snow ministers to shadows
the way a page accepts a hieroglyph.
From the eaves, the house depends icicles,
as if gaping up at the frigid moon.
And you are thinking of an absent friend,
a friend estranged by too much honesty,
or was it then too much dishonesty?
Quietly, you approach the thought, itself
a reproach, or a rapprochement with an
alienated moment you remember
now as the cause and not the effect, as
the whole and not the part. The figure of
speech, the stranger, waits for you to dream back
the memory you will own as your own.

Mere Islands

i
Block Island
Above, the red clay cliff, and above that,
a fringe of scrub grass and the overall sky.
Propped against great stones, boulders with ledges
streaked with quartz, we watch the sea roll in,
here, in the midst of the sea, where mere islands,
unmoved, move with the salted air and the sea.
  And in our ears, wind and words.

ii
Nantucket
The sea is the mother of islands: embraced
by isolation, by the overwhelming whelming—
seas heavy, sea placid—we are held by moods
we cannot affect, separate in our own contrivances.
On the jetty near the wharf, huddled in cold sunlight,
sheltered from the colder air, we open to another life.
  And in our ears, wind and words.

iii
Tahiti
In hot latitudes, the mother island left behind, a smaller,
offshore, before us: skies in the colors of a pencil set
turn over in easy days with a lazy latitude; noonness
pervades, the air moves to readjust the too perfect
picture of flowering trees and motu palms:

like that book between us, it beggars description.
            And in our ears, wind and words.

iv
Fiji
Here: ragged trees, fronds dried out to the point
of menace, stricken, like the island itself, by another
sort of poverty, the lush greenness of growing
beyond support, where the mere mention of the sea
is like an insult—that proximate, enduring plight,
that ugly real at the heart of beauty.
            And in our ears, wind and words.

v
Australia
Island nation, island people—we are both:
the sea surrounds us on all sides, and washes up
into our dreams at night. We dream of it by day:
the image the shadow of the word, and the word
illumination of desire—mere mother sea of what
we are, or simply wish for, in this inseparate world.
            And in our ears, wind and words.

Flight from the Present

We moved along the narrowing road,
it was dusk and trees on either side heaved,
sighing at our journey. Later, the air broke
into a cold sweat at the news we received.

Our destination could no longer be said
to be our future, for the track—it was but
a track now—led on like an enchantment
of the feet, for which we knew no respite.

No destiny in our destination, you say?
We could laugh to think we were so grand
as to want either—for now we only speak
of what we cannot fail to understand.

Each outcrop obscuring the trail, each
leafless tree collapsed across the way,
every mud hole and swampy patch we
took as a sign of increasing disarray.

Yes, it's conceivable we were circling back
to the place we fled. But who would prefer
present injuries to those past if it meant
no turning aside, even from an error?

Red Death

Warwick, 1740

Another season of the Red Death—
   smallpox, measles, cholera—
better we had called it the White Death
   who brought it along with guns,
whiskey, trinkets, and New York money.
   So when she arrived that day,
with child in hand, holding out her hand,
   we filled it with corn bread, more
bribery than charity, warding
   off sickness, though feeling sick
enough at heart, if the truth be known—
   grant us that at least, though least
is what we did, the more's the pity.
   It was no surprise when next
she returned, in the spring, and alone.
   Another Red Death, no doubt.
But she hadn't come empty-handed:
   seeds, she carried, of a type
unknown to us, small, black, granular.
   We planted them in black dirt
and waited to see what corn or fruit
   would repay our attentions.
That summer, small yellow spikes came up
   and stalks grew, tall, broad-leafed.
In late August she came again—last time—
   just as the long folded buds

unwrapped into bloom: giant flowers—
   rose mallow—with five petals
the color of clouds at dawn and dusk.
   She came, but kept her distance,
and when she held out her hands we knew
   right away the crimson marks.

Clasp

On days like today—when viciousness
is all the news and even your comrades
put the boot heel to the throat—unless
you are a stone without a fault, cracks
appear along lines of stress.

You sit as if in prayer, hands clasped,
elbows on the table top, forehead pressed
to a double fist unfit to grasp.
Yet one hand is a comfort to the other,
the fingers embracing in a caress

like some couple long together suddenly
made tender by grief or joy or a moment's
recognition of their frailty:
that it won't always be as it is now—
the heart open, the mind closed to vagrancy.

Variations on a Stanza by Longfellow

The frost has descended,
the harvest is ended,
as morning shimmers
   among the dead.

The vines have shriveled,
their leaves disheveled,
the flowers blackened,
   the lifeblood bled.

The light is retreating,
the nights are entreating:
"Come to the darkness,
   comfort is here."

While days grow shorter,
from every quarter
the winds are swirling,
   a pulse of fear.

Rime on the clover—
the birds fly over—
a summer of dying
   leaves us alone.

O year departing,
the end is starting,
the blade of dismay
   cuts to the bone.

III

Under the Iron Rainbow

Outback before Dawn

i.m. Philip Hodgins

Crux once for the ultimate land of scars,
the Southern Cross, sliding down the sky,
flickers at the end of a ribbon of stars.

Night deepens the more you lift your gaze,
while in the east, another band of light,
and above it the morning star ablaze.

It is change we mean when we speak of time,
and night revolving into day repeats
its pattern of inevitable rhyme.

On the horizon, trees in silhouette
stand distinct and black like shadows thrown
on the wall of a cave behind a parapet.

Even without a wind, who could doubt
we are turning round as we stand still
in the dark, in the midst of a season of drought?

The first sounds the newest morning emits
echo off the buildings, as roosters crow
like classical stichomythic poets.

An ensemble of magpies tune up their throats
while closer, in the field, a singular
bird introduces discordant notes.

To the west, a shooting star, unfurled,
has left its trace, like a quark in a chamber,
a synapse fired in a possible other world.

As the stars fade out, the growing light reveals
a cloud bank low in the sky; a reddish tinge
awakens a sense of what the light conceals.

Before the sun dawns, the world dilates,
changing imperceptibly like the minute
hand of a delicate clock. Day breaks.

In the Penal Colony

Only the copied text thus commands the soul of him who is occupied with it.

Walter Benjamin

Tabula rasa, terra nullius, nihil ex nihilo—
how these blank forms of thought are inscribed
upon us by the copyists of the laws, our jailers!

We are everywhere in chains, long before
this bondage confirms it—look over there,
the warders at their games, playing by the rules.

There is always the hope of escape, you say,
but to escape the bounds of hope is a further
freedom now beyond mere justice or injustice.

The writs, by all rights, are the very terms
we endure with our bodies, upon our bodies.
We will be free one day, when we are as nothing.

For now, we tend these machines lovingly—
they are in our image, mechanical, anonymous.
If they were poems, we would copy them out by hand.

On the Murray

for Stephano
Mildura, 1995

Rising from heights rare in Australia, the Murray uncoils
like a great serpent on a journey cross-country, the long
line traversing, composing, all terrains—as if limning
the borders of at least three states of mind: call them the New,
the South, and the Victorian. The Murray's capaciousness
is legendary, and the flow, the flow draws tribute
wherever it appears, like a great poem endless in its
variations and surety. In America, we'd
call the Murray the Mississippi, but only a blues
player and Brodsky's cat are famous for it. Rivers are
like that: you never know who they are going to invoke.
The Murray: a river of work, cutting its way through time
and all resistance: here broad and reflecting, there deep and
gorgeous in confinement—scoriated limestone valleys
of imagination—and stillness, too, as in swampy
backwaters and billabongs, where the traveler, the river's
reader, can paddle about and muse on the curious
vicissitudes of Nature's Muse, who is also like a
river, only she is her own sole source of plenishment,
whereas the Murray—refreshed by loss—is both less and more.

Kakadu Memory

after the painting by Neville Pilven

The rock striated with red in a blue wash
anchors the corner of the scene, while the wild
grasses, a frenzy of the wind, urge on
the burning horizon's fall into night—
      or is it an apocalypse of morning?

We are stranded—not lost—out here at the edge,
on edge, waiting for the light to resume whatever
movement across the sky is intended for us.
The bleakness has yielded up desert colors
      and the emptiness fills with bird song.

Who would have guessed love was an angular stone,
a monolith dividing the frame like sudden memory?
You will have to live more lives before this becomes
palpable in the recessed pattern: the concealed figure
      caught in the improbable sheen of desire.

We could walk hand in hand here, dividing
the tall grasses, their fingers reaching up to carry
away whatever wells—so desperate are they for
moisture and forgiveness. But we are found by loss,
      and await the return of a saving night.

Under the Iron Rainbow

i.m. Osmar White

Hard living, with a hardened life, steel
in the wounded legs, the soul steeled—and now,
the ghostly knowledge of release, here, so far away.

Gregarious solitary—your words, one by one, thrown
into a hollow, that worship of the one deed from
which comes no blessing but a laming.

Too much to remember—so easily forgot—
we live in shadows like the shades we invoke,
under various skies, under the iron rainbow.

Concedo Nulli

In Anderlecht, the Maison d'Erasme
sits in an elegant courtyard as if
withdrawn from the vulgar world—*concedo*
nulli read the signet rings in hot wax.
Across the way, l'Église de Saint-Pierre
crumbles in disrepair, its scaffolding
empty, all work halted. The foundations,
undermined by traffic and time, subsist.
Through a side door I step inside just as
the choir begins afternoon practice.
Schoolchildren, instructed by the priest, sit
on wooden chairs in the nave. One boy walks
in late, apologizes, takes his place.
They sing a Latin Erasmus would have
smiled at, weakly. The church is cold, colder
than outside. It is entirely local,
while the Maison functions as a locale.
The humanist never left the Church, from
which he was always apart: wit, satire,
ridicule—even mortared stone can rot.
In the faltering voices rehearsing
the hymns, there is no irony—and if
the priest takes pleasure in the sound, as do
I seated by a pillar in shadows,
it is because for moments at a time
what's praised is neither knowledge nor folly,
but an absence we cannot account for.

At the Terminus

I knew nothingness by heart.

                        E. M. Cioran

The trains glide in, silent but for the crackle
of the third rail—the electric lifeline that is death
to touch. As the doors separate, the people—

still in motion—disembark as if
nothing special had happened, as if to arrive
was never the point of the journey.

Men in uniform push carts loaded with
empty boxes, while across the way, high
on the wall, the information board clicks

over, revolving black shutters frenetically.
Everyone's face here shines with an eclipse
of memory in which nothing's quite

recalled and yet everything's familiar.
Almost in choreograph, the passengers
merge and deflect like currents

eddying in an estuary—no one
pauses to take in the acrid odor
of blackened chestnuts or the doughy smell

of waffle stands redolent of someone's home
a lifetime ago. If this is the afterlife,
why the hurry along the platforms?

A sharp whistle somewhere—and everywhere
in echo—breaks the spell the way a sudden crack
in hard-won composure reveals corridors of pain.

Now the pace quickens perceptibly—there's
no time to waste. At the terminus, the trains
run on time, third rail of mortality.

Disciples Asleep at Gethsemane

And he took with him Peter and the two sons of Zebedee, and
began to be sorrowful and very heavy.

Matt. 26:37

i

I have dreamt a dream of fulfillment, of freedom:
she was an old woman, with a face like the moon,
first full with reflection, then new and dark, and then
we were in a garden and the fountains murmured
words I wanted so much to hear, but mixed suddenly
with harsher tones, with disappointment—a man's voice.
I don't deny it: I hold hard to my needs, myself.

ii

Who was I to be chosen? It was late, and I understood
so little—though that little after my own fashion,
and who am I not to be accounted as good as anyone else?
I slept, and in my sleep knew I slept, and dreamed of being
awake—it was enough, surely, for I had been chosen.
Three times he returned and spoke, but I enfolded him
into myself, hearing him say, "Sleep, and take your rest."

iii

There was a meal, a hymn, some wine, and I followed,
wanting to be part of it all. We climbed a hill where
the trees were silver in the darkness, and a wind sighed
about us. It seemed to speak to my heart, saying, "This is

more than you," and so I listened, and followed, knelt
and entered that voice. And then there were lights, a crowd,
confusion, a kiss, and a naked man running away into the dark.

Three times nothing—still nothing, and those
brought to keep faith sleep in the garden.
The master dead, the dream erodes from within,
and sweet hope is made sweeter by perversion:
when it comes down to one, it comes down.
The land is gall—nor milk, nor honey flow,
and false friends keep watch unawake.

Iconoclastics

The Heavenly Ladder of Johannes Climacus
                                    Byzantine icon, late twelfth century

Hammers, arrows, ropes, tongs, and sheep hooks:
black devils in miniature drag
sinners off the heavenly ladder—
already precarious enough,
depicted in the icon without
the technique of a stabilizing
perspective. "Many are called but few
are chosen" amended to "fewer
still make it to the top," where waits an
Orthodox Christ to draw the elect
over the sill of Heaven. That poor
fellow, six steps from eternal life,
yanked by a cartoon fiend with punk hair
taking him in tow as if walking
the dog—and that other one, ridden
down like a horse plunging a hillside,
arms spread as if in benediction:
such are the perilous paths of straits
and narrows. Above, the heavenly
hosts almost obscure one another
with their shiny halos: they look on
with utmost anxiety, as though

Heaven were no less stressful than Earth.
Opposite, at the bottom corner,
in a tight cavern under a hill,
the damned look on like a Greek chorus
dumfounded, as anxious as angels.
If you study the faces of these
ladder-day saints you might recognize
your own type, though one appears to have
no face at all. He's sure to make it.

ii
Das Neue Jerusalem

German Fraktur, nineteenth century

In this water-colored woodcut, a folk-art
version of the old image: the narrow path leading
upwards to the gate of Heaven, the broad way
horizontal and seductive culminating in the pit.
At each entrance, the emblematical figure.

But what is this third path that stepwise joins
the upper road yet soon diverges—though still
rising—reaching almost to the foundations
of the Heavenly City above before plummeting
with its figures to the unholy cave below?

The middle way is no way at all if redemption
is the goal. It is a sad text, this preaching, for
we approve the eccentric, the original, the odd
as representative of diverging freedom, just as
this print catches the eye for its peculiar genius.

This is not wisdom but belief, we say, believing
all the more strongly in our wisdom to know

the difference. And our version of the distended
fiend with gaping maw in hand-colored flames?
The tortured soul, the tortured soul.

iii
Untitled

Rothko, no. 116, 1969

Flecks of white—like floaters in an inverse eye
or stars in the blacker sky of another world—
mark an inconsolable landscape that hardly
consoled a dying man: pale foreground stretching
like a desert to the horizontal line of night,
the far edge of dream, and beyond it
the black we see when we close our eyes.

And the thin frame of white paint?
It opens up the vision, insists on the border
between us and what we behold: another horizon,
a perspective that leads to the vanishing point.

Preaching the Cross

Then shall they begin to say to the mountains, Fall on us; and to the
hills, Cover us. For if they do these things in a green tree, what shall
be done in the dry?

                                                        Luke 23:30–31

In the gallery, where everything is hung "on the line,"
the images draw you in to send you out again, but where
is the eye to rest, when all the art proclaims itself as "fine,"
and the off-white walls are as neutral as the air?
    For if they do these things in a green tree,
    What shall be done in the dry?

The wooden cross-beams complicate the space,
lifting the ceiling to a cathedral form,
while picture after picture depicts the place
where defeat became the transfigured norm.
    For if they do these things in a green tree,
    What shall be done in the dry?

The skylight in the roof, braced with two-by-fours,
sections the sky, framing the disembodied
tree top that wavers in wind the way a woman adores
an icon in a chapel: rocked by transcendent need.
    For if they do these things in a green tree,
    What shall be done in the dry?

As shadows cross the floor in intricate stratagems,
patrons stroll from one death to another, covetous

of their own good fortune. Closer now, Jerusalem's daughters cry, "Let the mountains fall and cover us!"

For if they do these things in a green tree,
What shall be done in the dry?

Q & A

Questioner: By now, everyone has a grievance
              honed to a fine point by the abrasions
              of long acquaintance. Are we stuck?

Angel: You will know progress by the number
              of people who are angry with you.

Questioner: Seeing is so partial—how will I know
              fullness, how will I empty my eyes?

Angel: It is a blessing to see so poorly—if
              your skin were transparent, how vulgar
              you would appear to one another: veins,
              ligaments, tissue, organs pulsing. How
              much worse to know motivation inside out.

Questioner: You see us thus?

Angel: Worse. You occupy
              a dump seeping effluvium. And yet
              you have no idea of your purity.

Questioner: Then
              it is true, children playing with boats
              at the pool's edge, couples walking aglow
              on the gravel path, the old woman feeding
              the stray cats in the park, all are hints

of what we might become, having lost
what once we were?

Angel: So we are told. We are
only angels and cannot look farther than
our own realm allows. Yes, there are those
few who appear kindled, but they are
unaccountable and they frighten us.

Questioner: Then you do not know our future?

Angel: We do not even know your past. We are
here as long as you are here, as long as
you seek to question yourself.

The Repentant Magdalen

after Georges de La Tour

We are hollowed out by death, as by life.
How many moments to balance the weight
of forgetfulness—that knowingness which
is fear of an unknowing, a darkness?

You stare at the image of your image
until the glass reflects back the room where
you sit, in judgment, in the wavering
light, looking for the life within the skull.

Your fingers probe the sockets, your lips taste
the salt of your own flesh: you are not what
you seem—or, what you seem is what you are,
but that is a penance the future holds.

The room darkens, a trick of light suspends
the painting as an image in the air.
Who now contemplates? To whom attribute
these dense tribulations, this self-flaring?

You—parabolic!—who exist beside
me here, touch the radiant cell of this
life, illumine me beyond reflection,
and make remorse the glass of what I am.

Lines Left at Shiprock

14 August 1996

Westward, wings of rock
enfold the setting sun
as the world tilts
towards the edge of night.

You have come this far
and still you think
your life will endure.

The James Dickey Contemporary Poetry Series

Edited by Richard Howard

Error and Angels
Maureen Bloomfield

Ripper!
Carl Jay Buchanan

Portrait in a Spoon
James Cummins

From the Bones Out
Marisa de los Santos

The Land of Milk and Honey
Sarah Getty

All Clear
Robert Hahn

Without a Witness
Stella Johnston

Drowned Lands
Paul Kane

A Taxi to the Flame
Vickie Karp

Growing Back
Rika Lesser

Hours of the Cardinal
Richard Lyons

Lilac Cigarette in a Wish Cathedral
Robin Magowan

Traveling in Notions: The Stories of Gordon Penn
Michael J. Rosen

United Artists
S. X. Rosenstock

The Threshold of the New
Henry Sloss

Green
Sidney Wade